Weather

Dona Herweck Rice

Consultant

Timothy Rasinski, Ph.D
Kent State University

Publishing Credits

Dona Herweck Rice, *Editor-in-Chief*

Lee Aucoin, *Creative Director*

Conni Medina, M.A.Ed., *Editorial Director*

Jamey Acosta, *Editor*

Robin Erickson, *Designer*

Stephanie Reid, *Photo Editor*

Rachelle Cracchiolo, M.S.Ed., *Publisher*

Based on writing from *TIME For Kids*.

TIME For Kids and the *TIME For Kids* logo are registered trademarks of TIME Inc.
Used under license.

Teacher Created Materials

5301 Oceanus Drive
Huntington Beach, CA 92649-1030
http://www.tcmpub.com

ISBN 978-1-4333-3575-4

© 2012 Teacher Created Materials, Inc.

What is the
weather today?
How do you know?

Is it warm and sunny?

Is it cold and
snowy?

Is it wet and rainy?

Is it cool and cloudy?

Is it dry and windy?

Is it dark and foggy?

How do you know the weather?

See it in the sky.
Feel it on your skin.

Words to Know

and	rainy
cloudy	see
cold	skin
cool	sky
dark	snowy
do	sunny
dry	the
feel	today
foggy	warm
how	weather
in	wet
is	what
it	windy
know	you
on	your